Rhinos

by Helen Orme

ticktock

Copyright © ticktock Entertainment Ltd 2006
First published in Great Britain in 2006 by ticktock Media Ltd.,
Unit 2, Orchard Business Centre, North Farm Road,
Tunbridge Wells, Kent, TN2 3XF
ISBN 1 84696 083 5 pbk
Printed in China

We would like to thank our consultants: The International Rhino Foundation -
www.rhinos-irf.org/savetherhinos

Picture credits
t=top, b=bottom, c=centre, l-left, r=right
Corbis: 1, 2, 9, 14, 15, 18, 19, 22-23, 25, 27, 28, 29, 31, 32. Oxford Scientific Photo Library: 8b.
Shutterstock: OFC, 4-5, 6-7, 8t, 10-11, 12-13, 16-17, 20-21, 22-23, 26. Superstock: 7b, 10, 17t.
Every effort has been made to trace the copyright holders, and we apologise in advance for any unintentional omissions.
We would be pleased to insert the appropriate acknowledgements in any subsequent edition of this publication.

CONTENTS

Words that appear **in bold** are explained in the glossary.

AN ANIMAL IN DANGER

Rhino is short for rhinoceros, which means 'nose horn'. There are five different types of rhino.

African rhinos live on the grassy plains of southern Africa. Asian rhinos live in forests and on grasslands in India and other countries in South East Asia.

All types of rhino are endangered. Some are very close to disappearing completely.

An Asian female rhinoceros and her calf.

An African bull (male) rhinoceros.

5

AFRICAN RHINOS

Two sorts of rhino live in Africa, the Black rhino and the White rhino. Both types are actually the same colour – grey!

African rhinos live on open plains, called the **savannah**. They are plant eaters. They eat grass and leaves from low-growing bushes.

The African name for White rhinos was wide mouthed rhinos, because they have wider mouths than the Black rhinos. People who came to Africa thought the local people said white, not wide, and this is how they got their name.

An African White rhino

BLACK RHINO FACT

Black rhinos are the rarest African rhino. Many of them are now in **wildlife reserves** where they are looked after and guarded. Without this help, they would disappear very quickly.

ASIAN RHINOS

There are three sorts of rhinos living in Asia. These are the Indian, Sumatran and Javan rhino.

Indian rhinos live in open places, near rivers in the north of India and in Nepal.

An Indian rhino

The Sumatran rhino lives in forests in Borneo and Sumatra. It is sometimes called the hairy rhinoceros because it is has a shaggy coat of hair.

JAVAN RHINO

The Javan rhino is the rarest of all the rhinos. There are only about 60 animals left in the world. They live in Java and Vietnam.

A hairy Sumatran rhino

FEEDING

All rinos are **herbivores**, but different sorts of rhinos eat in different ways.

Grazers, such as the White rhinos in this picture, eat grass and other plants found on the ground.

Browsers, like the Black rhino, eat leaves growing on bushes and trees.

Grazers and browsers have different shaped mouths. Wide mouths are good for grazing. Narrow, pointed lips are best for browsing.

A black rhino's mouth is the right shape for browsing.

RHINO LIFE

Adult rhinos usually live alone. They come together for mating and sometimes White rhinos will gather where there is lots of food or water.

If you see a group of rhinos, it is most likely to be a mother with her young, or a small group of females.

In this picture, female rhinos are cooling off in a waterhole with their calves.

Male rhinos have **territories**. They mark them with piles of dung. Sometimes these are a metre high! This is a warning to other male rhinos to stay away.

Male rhinos will fight other male rhinos that come into their territory.

CHARGING RHINOS

Many people think that rhinos are dangerous animals. They think rhinos will charge at people or vehicles for no reason.

This isn't true. But if a rhino is frightened by people or another animal, it can run fast – up to 50 kilometres an hour!

A group of rhinos is called a 'crash' of rhinos. Maybe this is because they 'crash' through trees and bushes when they are running.

A White rhino with her calf.

White and Indian rhino calves usually run in front of their mothers. The calves of Black, Javan and Sumatran rhinos run behind their mothers.

PROBLEMS FOR RHINOS – HORNS

Black and White rhinos and Sumatran rhinos have two horns. Indian and Javan rhinos have one horn.

Male rhinos use their horns when they are fighting over territories. The front horn of a male White rhino can grow to 1.3 metres long.

Some people use rhino horn to make medicines. They believe that rhino horn can cure illnesses – but this isn't true!

Rhino horn is also used to make dagger handles, called 'jambiya', in Yemen, Asia.

Many rhinos have been killed for their horns. **Poaching** is the main reason why these animals are endangered.

RHINO HORN

Rhino horns are made of keratin. This is the same stuff that your fingernails are made of. Like your fingernails, rhino horns are no use in medicine at all!

Rhinos in a wildlife reserve
with park wardens who
guard them.

PROBLEMS FOR RHINOS – HABITAT LOSS

*In Africa and in Asia the human **population** is growing. More and more land is needed to grow food for people.*

Rhinos need a large area of land to find enough food to eat. Their **habitat** is being taken over and used for farming.

Most rhinos now have to live in protected **wildlife reserves**.

In Asia, the Sumatran rhinos are losing their habitat, too. The forests where they live are being cut down by **illegal loggers**.

PROBLEMS FOR RHINOS – CLIMATE CHANGE

The changing climate could be a big problem for rhinos and other wild animals.

Climate change can cause **droughts**. Rhinos are put at risk if waterholes dry up. They have to travel long distances to find water, and might not find enough to survive!

When there is less rain, the sorts of plants that grow change. In Africa, the grasses that some rhinos eat might be replaced by scrubby bushes.

Less rain also means that desert areas with no plants at all will get bigger.

SAVING THE RHINO

People are trying very hard to save the rhino.

Zoos around the world have set up **breeding programmes** for rhinos.

In Africa and Asia wildlife reserves are meant to be safe homes for rhinos. Even so, sometimes poaching still happens.

One way to save the rhino is for **tourists** to visit the animals to watch them in their natural habitat.

Wildlife tourism brings in money for the countries where rhinos live. This means protecting the rhinos is important to local people.

FACTFILE

WHERE DO RHINOS LIVE?

The red areas on the maps show where rhinos live.

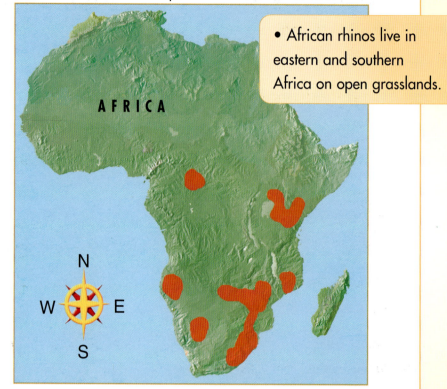

• African rhinos live in eastern and southern Africa on open grasslands.

• Indian rhinos live in open areas in northern India and southern Nepal.

• Sumatran and Javan rhinos live in small areas of Nepal, Malaysia and Indonesia in swamps and forests.

RHINO BODIES

White rhinos are the biggest of all the rhinos. After the elephant, they are the biggest land-living mammals.

THE BIGGEST:

White rhino

Length: up to 4 metres
Height: up to 1.8 metres
Weight: up to 2500 kilograms

THE SMALLEST:

Sumatran rhino

Length: up to 3 metres
Height: up to 1.5 metres
Weight: up to 800 kilograms

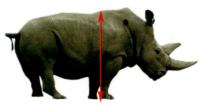

• Both male and female rhinos have horns.

• A rhino's biggest muscles are in its neck. These big muscles are needed to hold up the rhino's huge head.

• Rhino skin looks tough, but it can be damaged by the sun and insect bites. Rhinos keep their skins covered in mud to protect them.

25

RHINO CALVES

• Rhino mothers have their first babies (called calves) when they are about eight years old. After that they can have calves once every two to four years.

• Rhinos only have one baby at a time.

• The male rhinos do not help to bring up the calves.

• The baby rhinos stay with their mothers for at least two years.

• If a predator such as a crocodile or lion comes near, a mother rhino will protect a young calf by standing over it.

RHINO LIFE AND FOOD

- Rhinos spend most of their life finding food and drinking at waterholes.

- Grazers, such as White rhinos and Indian rhinos, eat grass and other ground plants.

- Browsers, such as Sumatran, Javan and Black rhinos eat leaves from trees and bushes.

- Rhinos have poor eyesight, but a very good sense of smell. They use smell to recognise each other, to find food and to keep out of danger.

- Adult rhinos have no natural **predators**. In the wild, a rhino can live to be 40 years old.

- The rhino's best friend is the tick bird. This bird sits on the rhino and eats any insects on the rhino's skin.

FACTFILE

RHINOS IN DANGER

Animal experts believe that 200 years ago there were over 1 million rhinos in the world.

Now there are fewer than 18,700.

HOW MANY RHINOS	
TYPE	**Number left today**
White rhinos	12,000
Black rhinos	3700
Indian rhinos	2550
Sumatran rhinos	300
Javan rhinos	60

- Even though it is against the law to kill rhinos, poaching is still happening.

- Rhinos are killed for their horns which people believe can cure illnesses.

- Rhino horn can be worth more than gold.

- Rhinos are also in danger from habitat loss. Their habitat is wanted by people to use as farmland. Forest rhinos are losing their habitat because the forests are cut down for wood.

- There is some good news. The number of rhinos is going up slightly – but only in some areas.

CONSERVATION

• Wildlife reserves have been set up in Africa and India. Some reserves have strong fences to keep poachers out and the animals in. But even in the reserves poaching still happens.

• Sometimes wildlife reserves use land that local people would like to use to grow food. One way to help people and the animals live together is to involve local people in wildlife tourism. People love to see animals living in the wild. These tourists need hotels and transport. They might also buy craft objects to take home. This means that there is work and money for local people.

• Some groups of rhinos have guards with guns to look after them. But some poachers will even kill the guards to get at the rhinos.

• **Conservationists** can cut off a rhino's horns under anaesthetic. This doesn't hurt the rhino – it's a bit like cutting your fingernails. If the rhino's horns are gone, there is no reason for poachers to kill it. Sometimes conservationists insert radio transmitters into rhinos' horns. This helps them to track the rhinos and find the animals if they are injured or have been attacked.

HOW YOU CAN HELP RHINOS

• Join an organisation like the *World Wildlife Fund*. They need to raise money to pay for their conservation work. You could organise an event to help raise funds – try having a sale of all your unwanted clothes, old toys and books! You can also give money to the *Save the Rhinos* campaigns (see below). The money goes directly to help protect rhinos.

• Find out about schemes that let you adopt or foster a rhino. (Don't worry – it won't have to live at your house!) See the *Adopt Wildlife* and *David Sheldrick Wildlife Trust* websites below.

• Be a good conservationist. Look after the place where you live. There are some good ideas to help you on the *Go Wild!* section of the *World Wildlife Fund* website and the education section of the *IRF* website.

Visit these websites for more information and to find out how you can help to 'Save the rhinos'.

International Rhino Foundation: www.rhinos-irf.org/savetherhinos www.savetherhino.org

The Adopt Wildlife website: www.adoptwildlife.org

The David Sheldrick Wildlife Trust www.sheldrickwildlifetrust.org

World Wildlife Fund International: www.wwf.org.uk

breeding programmes Zoos keep rare animals. They help them breed by giving them mates and they help to look after the babies. Many zoos try to put the animals they breed back into the wild, if it is safe.

climate change When the weather in an area changes and stays changed. For example, an area which once had lots of rain may become very dry.

conservationists People who take care of the natural world. Conservationists try to stop people hunting endangered animals and they ask governments to pass laws to protect wild habitats.

droughts When there is no rain for a very long time.

habitat The place that suits a particular animal or plant, in the wild.

herbivores Animals that live by eating plants.

illegal loggers People who cut down trees without permission to sell them for wood. They destroy large areas of forest habitat.

poaching The capturing or killing of animals by poachers so that they, or parts of their bodies, can be sold.

population The people who live in a particular place or country.

predators Animals that live by killing and eating other animals.

savannah A large, open area of land in Africa where grasses and bushes grow.

territories Areas of land that one animal, and its family, believes is its own home and its area for finding its food.

tourists People who are on holiday.

wildlife reserves Places set aside for wild animals and plants to live. The animals and their habitat are protected by laws.

INDEX